Welcome

1099 Economy: build your personal economy

By Ericka S. Williams

Dedication

Thanks for stepping up to the future. 1099 lifestyle is the future of jobs, the US economy and worldwide services. If you are reading this book feel free to move around chapters, and use this book to help someone recently unemployed or fresh out of college as well. You can take your personal economy in your hands.

I want to thank my mom who 20+ years of military service and repeat deployments encouraged my journey to this day. To my nieces and nephews who have seem me run businesses, struggle, and try to stay true, I want you to know the sky is the limit.

Table of Contents

1. Why 1099 lifestyle
2. Immigrants Number 1 business creators. Why?
3. Making 100,000 a year possible.
4. Automation is your best friend
5. Apps to use to invest through automation
6. Investing in Real estate in as little as $1000-$5000 dollars.
7. Why Now
8. Inequality growing because of lack of knowledge
9. What's happening to jobs
10. Less workers needed
11. Why its easier than ever to start a company
12. Driver contracts
13. Service companies
14. Administrative
15. Online business
16. Ebooks/online programs
17. Consulting
18. Honey
19. Coffee
20. Body butters

21. Natural Hair /hair care Products/ Product based companies
    a. Men hair care
    b. Organic anything
    c. Vitamins
    d. Herbalife millionaires
    e. Usana millionaires
    f. Energy drink
    g. Amazon
    h. Ebay
    i. Craigslist
22. Building your personal economy
23. Farmland
24. Timber
25. Rental income
26. Precious metals
27. Dividend income
28. Profit income
29. Earned income
30. Insurance
31. Tax writeoffs
32. Live well and teach others
33. Teach 10 others

Chapter 1

Why 1099 lifestyle

What is the 1099 lifestyle? It's the full time living from nontraditional means. You could be a uber driver, an independent contractor for small to large size companies and full time business owner.

Leaving 9-5 lifestyle can be hard. For some it's a not by choice. The average job life span is 2.5 years. This means many Americans will be changing jobs frequently. Why not take greater control of your life and income.

This book will help you build streams of income through ways you may not heard before. The economy is changing quickly and you need to be flexible. I will share with you why now is more important than ever.

70% of people dissatisfied with jobs why do people stay in jobs they hate and causes them sickness, headaches, and heart attacks. (http://www.geekwire.com/2013/study-70-americans-jobs/)

60% of college students cannot find jobs in their major. You need networking and sales skills. Every company needs sales skills. Make yourself different from the pack. 80% of jobs are found from referrals, and who you know. Many companies do not want to go through the hassle of being drowned in thousands of resumes and taking time from their work to do interviews. On top of that the training. This is why I wrote volunteer to 6 figures book. Its important for you to volunteer where you can meet different types of people within different companies.

You must network and when someone ask what are you currently doing volunteering and bettering yourself.

80% of foreclosures could have been avoided if families had brought in an extra $1,000/month during the housing crisis. What would you do with an extra $1,000/ month on top of what you already make? What bills could you eliminate by implementing a plan that brought an extra $1,000/month into your household? I really want to know what people need. It's time to put more people in winning positions.

Companies letting people go and using temp workers more and more. Its cost effective not as much as attachment. The company doesn't have to pay insurance and benefits but gets an eager worker.

Over 6000 US retailers are closing their doors in the next 4 years.

(http://www.zerohedge.com/news/2015-05-02/major-us-retailers-are-closing-more-6000-stores)

All the jobs you would send your teenagers and part time job for your college student are going to be gone. Many things are changing out over to online stores and sales.

223 Barnes & Noble (through 2023) which makes me extremely sad, because I remember all the free reading I did at Barnes and Nobles. The excitement of having a extra 20 dollars in my pocket to grab a book for the week. It's important to feed your mind new information. Blogs, magazines and other items. It just shows how powerful amazon is for books and other sites are for text books.

340 Dollar Tree/Family Dollar. Dollar tree and family door works with lower income families and lower income areas. It's increasing to see them taking a hit.

400 Office Depot/Office Max (by 2016) Mergers sometimes cause stores to close. I have a feeling this is due to the strong purchasing power of online office shopping.

1,784 Radio Shack Radio Shack has been a confused and limp shark in the water for many years at this point. I think its remaining stores have been in the Midwest. Which is same for the Midwest areas.

200 Walgreens (by 2017) this is why you should support the small town pharmacist because we have given way to CVS and Walgreens paying pharmacists pennies and now they will be closing. As well as not all prescriptions can be mail to your door. The risk of the thief would scare me away from mailing prescriptions to an elderly person's home anyways.

Is it time to switch over to the side passion you been having? Sometimes our passions do not pay well or so we think. Is it computer related, service related, have you checked out the possibility of it becoming a 6 figure income?

Ready to take your life to the next level? So many Americans are not living the full dream of their lives. Write down some of your current dreams and what you will have to give up to get there.

W.I.M.P = Where is my paycheck

Tired of waiting on a paycheck? I know realtors and commission saleswomen and men a like that get into ruts when checks don't come weekly. Why? Because it means you need to increase your sales frequency so that checks are being at your door. As well pouring money into different monthly dividend stocks, real estate ventures and lending club so that different checks are running into my account at any given time. Learning how to create streams of income or paychecks into your mailbox.

No free time in the morning to spend with your family? I remember watching a Amway video (yes I know Amway, hold your judgement) the guy was eating pancakes with his children in the mornings and holding a sign by the highway in traffic that says "only 40 more years." Oh course he probably drove folks crazy with the sign. But the sign was important. It was that jarring moment while you are in traffic desiring to be somewhere else or taking a vacation you were there in traffic. How important is it for you to spend time with you kids? With your spouse? No time to vacation? The average American only takes about 16 days a year. I feel that average is a little high. What is it really saying is people take a few sick days, thanksgiving and Christmas. Is this how you want to live? Barely getting a few days with your family? Wish you could carve out your personal economy to spend more times with spouse, kids and doing the things you love. 16 days is just not enough. I could say the French and Germans take it too far with 6-8 weeks of paid time off but it works for their country.

Ready to break out of the financial cap placed over you by a **JOB**? Job is jokingly called **Just Over Broke**. DO not get me wrong most of the time jobs are great things it can bring self-esteem and a roof over your head. The reason it's just over broke is because most people fill out their w4 WRONG. That's why I like the guys at **Myecon** that's all they specialize in fixing your w4. **Why is it so important? 1/3 of all your income goes to state and federal taxes**. I know some of you may argue about which state is better trust me this is an average of what every single American pays.

Laid off? Fired? Ready to take your life in your own hands. It's the worst feeling, getting fired. I know a friend who worked his tail off for 6 years building this small company up to a big name in the area. It's crazy he knocked on **10,000 business doors in the Texas area**. Guess what? The company doesn't care about you. It just doesn't. I know people fighting me tooth and nail about their company and how great it is. These same people will be shocked and heart broken when that same company goes PEACE out. That's the sad part if you could focus 10x the energy into themselves and their side income life would be different.

Chapter 2

Immigrants Number 1 business creators. Why?

"The truth is, immigrants tend to be more American than people born here."
— Chuck Palahniuk, Choke

Being loyal to a company is twofold. I want you on your job giving it a 100% but when you get home I want you to focus on that 5-9pm. **Immigrants come here and work on their 5-9pm from day one.** There is just too much opportunity here. That's why we hear so many success stories from immigrants who come here with nothing.

Immigrants account for 13% of the U.S. population; however, over the last two decades immigrant owned businesses have made up 30% of the growth in the small business economy, which makes up nearly a third of private-sector employment. One in six small-business owners in the U.S. is an immigrant. (http://xpatnation.co/self-made-immigrant-success-stories/#.X73G70I9q) Perfect example is Forever 21 creators Of course, the couple didn't always had it easy: After moving to America from Korea in 1981, Do Won had to work three jobs at the same time to make ends meet. According to Forbes, **Do Won Chang worked as a janitor, gas station attendant, and in a coffee shop when he first moved to America.** Do Won decided on a retail career while pumping gas, one of several jobs he juggled as a new immigrant. Of course, the retail career later turned into the fashion brand Forever 21.

The couple had been in the States for only three years when the company opened their first store in Highland Park, California, a neighborhood located about five minutes north of downtown Los Angeles. The store produced approximately $700,000 during its first year and still remains in the same location to this day. (https://vulcanpost.com/3736/from-rags-to-riches-the-story-behind-forever-21-cofounders/)

Sergey Brin – Born in Moscow Russia, Sergey Brin's father sought to move to the United States. He felt his Jewish heritage was preventing him from studying physics as further education during a difficult time for the Soviet Union. (The Google Story) Russia's loss was America's gain, Michael Brin went on to teach mathematics at the University of Marlyand while Genia Brin, Sergey's mother worked as a researcher for NASA. Sergey grew up to found Google, a company with a 400 billion dollar market cap and true global reach and revenue. While American R&D and the set up Sergio found himself in with university facilities and venture capital played a vital part in the Google story, there is no question that Google would not be the Google we know today without the man hours and brilliance that Sergey Brin brought to the table.

George Soros -26.5B – The divisive billionaire is best known for his political affiliations, heavily involved with financing recent democratic candidates, liberal think tanks and organizations. George Soros was born in Budapest Hungary and made a fortune in currency speculation and bond trading. Even though his financial services companies have never been massive employers (compared to others on this list) and he is currently set up with a family office, his firms have made plenty of money for many American investors and funds.

His $26.5 billion net worth will have included huge tax payments, his line of business has also resulted in large sums of money being made from foreign countries and brought back to the United States. He is known for his generous philanthropy.

In a 2007 Time magazine article it was noted that he had given away at least $7 billion including over $742 million within America. Along with helping to pay for infrastructure that helps with internet freedom and dealing with poverty and education in Africa.

Len Blavatnik, Ukraine 21.8B Another

immigrant that is America's gain and Russia's loss. Len was born in the USSR in Odessa Ukraine. Also struggling with further education due to his Jewish heritage and his family's request for an exit visa. Len's fortune primarily is focused around 3 business sectors, Raw materials, Chemicals and Media and Communication. Founding Access Industries in 1986 he spends his wealth investing and donating towards culture and the arts, and has an impressive collection of real estate.

Rupert Murdoch, Australia $12.5B. Born in 1931 in Melbourne Australia, Rupert became a naturalized US citizen in 1985. Perhaps the most influential immigrant in America, Rupert Murdoch's Newscorp is heavily involved in Media and Communication in America as well as the UK, Canada and his native Australia. In America his companies the New York Post, Wall Street Journal and Fox News show a heavy right leaning political tendency, he also owns some left leaning papers across the globe, as well as famously supporting the left wing Labour party in the UK for over a decade up until a dramatic change of direction when supporting Conservative David Cameron in the past election. News Corp employs nearly 50,000 people world wide, with it's largest market being the United States. Rupert is also highly influential across Hollywood, his production house 21st Century Fox has annual revenues of over $27 billion (2013) with hits such as Avatar, co production with Marvel studios for a host of comic book blockbusters and of course The Simpsons. Patrick Soon-Shiong, $11.9B Born in Port Elizabeth South Africa to Chinese parents, Patrick is known as both the richest American in the healthcare industry and the richest man in Los Angeles. He has built and sold two pharmaceutical companies, and developed drugs that focus on America's difficult diabetes problems. He too has donated generously, according to the board of directors page at the Healthcare transformation institute he pledged US $1 billion to support healthcare transformation and a national health information highway. He also guaranteed $100 million to reopen the Martin Luther King hospital in south LA.

Pierre Omidyar, France Ebay $8BAnother immigrant tech entrepreneur, Pierre and his family made their way to America via France, where Pieere was born to Iranian immigrant parents. He earned a degree in computer science from Tufts university and founded Ebay in 1995 taking it public in 1998 making him a billionaire at the tender age of 31. He has invested in media, launching the successful Honolulu Civil Beat which has been voted the best newspaper in Hawaii 3 years running. in 2014 he launched First look media and boasts experienced and ground breaking Pulitzer surprise winning journalists Glenn Greenwald and Laura Poitras who worked on and broke the Edward Snowden story for the UK's Guardian Newspaper.

Elon Musk, $9.6B. Born in 1971 in South Africa to a Canadian mother and South African father, Elon moved to America in 1992 to study physics at the University of Pennsylvania. He later started the company called x.com which merged with a holding company that owned Paypal. Elon Musk became a key member in the now infamous PayPal Mafia. He is perhaps now most famous for his ambitious projects in the form of SpaceX. A company

that manufactures and launches space rockets, with the long term goal of allowing Human kind to live on other planets. He has also had tremendous success with his electric car company Tesla Motors, which is not only on its way to transforming the way Americans drive but is well on the way to massively changing the way energy is stored with his recent $5 billion investment into a Nevada battery factory.
In philanthropy, Musk makes use of his technical expertise and connections to finance and donate Solar panels to areas of environmental disaster. Lending support to a hurricane response center in Alabama after the city was left short supplied in 2010, and to Soma city in Fukishima Japan to help with relief efforts. He has signed on to the Bill and Melinda Gates "The Giving Pledge" to agree to give up the majority of his wealth to philanthropic causes.

David Sun, Taiwan, $4.8B worth an estimated $4.8 billion mostly from the business he co-founded called Kingston Technology, which makes memory products for Laptops, Desktops, servers and printers as well as Flash memory for Cell phones. Although Kingston industries is in decline due to the rise of non flash based mobile technology, it still employees over 4100 people many, high earning engineers at their Fountain Valley CA headquarters.

Thomas Peterffy, $9.4B born in Hungary in a hospital shelter during Russian bombing, Thomas moved to New York not speaking a word of English, working at an engineering firm building highways, he volunteered to program a newly purchased computer and this had an effect on his future. as he moved into the financial markets, specializing in financial modelling software and founding discount brokerage firm Interactive Brokers.

Officially a registered independent, his youth in socialist Hungary has lead him to be a stanch backer of the republican party, he ran much publicized commercials talking about his story and escape from socialist Hungary to America, but refused to back any Super Pacs believing them to be too extreme. "The reason I didn't join a PAC is because I'm politically moderate and most PACs are not," Peterffy said. "My political orientation is not fitting with any of the Republican PACs."
(http://xpatnation.co/10-most-financially-successful-immigrants-in-america/#.068R70a6V)

Vinod Dham, the "Father of Pentium"Born in Pune, India, Dham came to the U.S. in 1975 as an engineering student with just $8 in his pocket.Thanks to a loan from the University of Cincinnati's study abroad office, Dham was able to make it through his studies and upon graduation began to work for Intel, helping to invent the first flash memory chip. He went on to become the CEO of Silicon Spice, which sold for $1.2 billion in 2002. He is now a venture capitalist, and is looking to give back to his native country.

Lowell Hawthorne, founder of Golden Krust Caribbean Bakery & GrillHawthorne left behind his family's bakery in Jamaica and emigrated to the U.S. He found employment with the NYPD and after ten years of accounting he decided he wanted to return to baking. He pooled money from family members and his savings to launch Golden Krust in 1989 in the Bronx. Today, Golden Krust can be found in 125 franchises in nine states along the Eastern seaboard, and grosses more than $100 million in annual sales.

Hawthorne says his success depended on serving its primary customer — the Caribbean community. It also would not have succeeded without strong family support.

From all these examples you see what is possible for you as American. How you are born here with more advantages then most. Get a head start teach your kids, and others looking for work. It's time to get ahead in American you have the leg up as far as opportunity. It's not if you can start a side business, or become an independent contractor it's when and how. Remember people are swimming, sneaking into and signing up for thousands in college debt to have the opportunity to be in America.

Chapter 3

Making 100,000 a year possible.

"How much money do I need to make?" you'll say, "What do I want to do with my life—and how can I use money to do it?"
— Ramit Sethi, I Will Teach You To Be Rich

Possibility to make 100-300 dollars a day bringing you to 109,000 a year income. When a friend said it's his daily goal to reach $300 dollars a day. I had one entrepreneur I interviewed OD Harris of OD Harris Media say you will work on average 2400 hours a year now if you want to be a millionaire or make a million dollars each hour $416. Imagine the difference in saying you need $300 a day to you shouldn't be making less than $400 dollars an hour. I know it's a little early for me to expect you to make $400 dollars an hour, but I am 100% serious about you aiming for $300 a day. If you drive for Uber, Lyft, Ride Share, Instacart, sell on amazon, sell on craigslist/ebay, sell on your personal blog/YouTube channel/website. That is 6 opportunities to just make $75 dollars each opportunity. I know many people making at least $3,000-$5,000 dollars a month doing Uber/Lyft alone. If you can make a program or product on your website for $97 dollars you just have to sell 3 a day, or a $197 you could just sell one product a day. By combining different options you can quickly reach your goal. This is what the 1099 lifestyle is about creating a personal economy for yourself. Eventually you will be able to remove yourself from the actual trading time for dollars model by the end of the book.

Chapter 4

Automation is your best friend.

Best way to invest income is through automation. I am a big believer in automation. Willpower fades over time. I use to work at Lowes Home Improvement people worked there for 10 or more years and not saving any money for retirement. It was the saddest thing I have ever seen. Lowes Home Improvement decide it had to do what was best for its employees so they forced a 1% saving and 1% company match of your retirement funds. Lowes matching up to 6% but many folks refuse to even address it. There was a manager with 3 million dollars in retirement right before Lowes bought back a 1/3 of its stock making "Larry big mouth manager." Going from 3 million to 1 million dollars overnight.

There is what the problem Larry had faith in investing as the company said but no ideas on how to invest his money outside of Lowes. This resulted Mr Larry (totally fake name) having to work many more years for Lowes. I meet many more just like him working 10 or more years for Lowes with $50,000 to $100,000 saved up but no clue what to do with it.

There are apps I suggest people use. Accorn App and Digit.co app. The first app is an investment app putting your money into a mutual fund of your choice. And the digit.co is a savings app that helps you grow your savings. I think both are great for you not being able to keep willpower going 24/7.

Another thing I would recommend is having an Etrade account and every Thursday when deposits reach your account you take 10% off the top. Uber, Lyft, Instacart and many other 1099 companies all pay on Thursday. I think it's wise before most people have that Friday just got paid mentality. It keeps you contracting for work because you will need more funds.

I suggest it going right into dividend stocks. I use dividend.com myself its very helpful. I only focus on stocks that pay monthly because I can keep track if I a deposit has reached my account. Most people think and would suggest you do reinvesting of your dividends. I like to see it in the account first because it lets me know or enforce how much more I need to put in.

Chapter 5

Apps to use to invest through automation

"The single most important factor to getting rich is getting started, not being the smartest person in the room."
— Ramit Sethi, I Will Teach You To Be Rich

There are apps I suggest people use. Accorn App and Digit.co app. The first app is an investment app putting your money into a mutual fund of your choice. And the digit.co is a savings app that helps you grow your savings. I think both are great for you not being able to keep willpower going 24/7.

MOTIF investing

Motif investing is low cost themed diversification. You will need a 250 dollar investment to start investing.

A review of the Motif Investing website below: Each motif features between 20 to 30 stocks or ETFs that can be said to follow particular themes. Examples include "Healthy and Tasty," "Utility Bills," "Recession Resistant," and "Biotech Breakthroughs." There is even a "Lots of Likes" motif that focuses on companies with the most Likes on Facebook. It's an interesting twist on the theme of "asset allocation," since you can choose from a number of different "asset classes" to create a one-of-a-kind portfolio.

You can look for motifs using different criteria, such as exploring by industry or looking for themes based on current events. It's also possible to screen motifs by looking at daily change, one year return, and popularity. The screener allows you the chance to find just what you're looking for in an investment. Motif Investing is quite cost-efficient as well. **You get access to each of the stocks in the motif for one flat fee of $9.95 per transaction.** No matter how much you customize a motif. There are no management fees, and no activity requirements. However, the fact that you can get 30 stocks or ETFs at once, for less than $10, is a big deal. Anytime you trade a motif; you just pay the flat transaction fee. (http://investorjunkie.com/15548/motif-investing-review/)

Chapter 6

Investing in Real estate in as little as $1000-$5000 dollars.

"On average, millionaires invest 20 percent of their household income each year."
— Ramit Sethi, I Will Teach You To Be Rich

There are over 50 real estate crowdfunding sites in the USA. I think they are amazing some states are creating paperwork to make sure everyone is an accredited investor. Thank GOD for Texas residency, I am able to invest with Realty Shares with as little as $1000-$5000 dollars. I then own a piece of a commercial building, residential building or other projects in which I will be paid a monthly dividend as a shareholder.

You can also invest as little as $1,000-$5000 in some homes in south east many homes going for $25,000-$50000 dollars making some of your owner occupant loans, USDA loans. USDA loans are 100% financed where all you are paying are closing costs. I strongly suggest you get to understanding Airbnb and getting roommates so you can live rent free.

If you are leaving college and getting nowhere "job" hunting, do not move in with your parents. Here is a way to create your future to be opposite of your peers.

Chapter 7

Why now

"Why climb the corporate ladder when you can build an elevator in your own building?"
— Joshua E. Leyenhorst

Companies are switching to independent contractors, time warner, cable providers, everyone. If you were to just google independent contractors it's everywhere. There opportunity to go full time profit in this field is endless. You can grow the opportunity for yourself or wait for a "perfect" job with full time benefits to appear. Over 23 million Americans are self-employed in the USA according the US Census. I numbers I see on business insider are 53 million people. Which means some folks have not fully transitions to calling themselves a full time business.

"It's not your employer's job to make you rich it's your job to make you rich." Jim Rohn

Chapter 8

Inequality growing because of lack of financial knowledge.

"It is not inequality which is the real misfortune, it is dependence."
— Voltaire

With income inequality at its worst in the US since the 1920s and President Barack Obama calling widening income inequality the "defining challenge of our time," there has been an expansive push to address the issue.

In a new report, Causes and Consequences of Income Inequality: A Global Perspective, the IMF aims to show why policymakers need to focus more on the poor and the middle class. The report determined that income inequality and income distribution matter for growth and its sustainability in a country.(http://finance.yahoo.com/news/study-shows-inequality-growing-most-131400745.html)

Why is inequality growing so much no one is taught personal finance any more. After 1905 when John Rockfeller took personal finance and accounting out of the public school system people have been getting into ridiculous debt ever since.

In the future I want to do 2-4 hour workshops on business creation and personal finance. People just do not understand how bad high interest is. How easy it is to restart your credit.

Chapter 9

What's happening to jobs?

"Recessions are the best time to start a company. Companies fail. Others hold back capital. If you are willing to do the preparation and work, it is the best time to invest in yourself and start a business." -- Mark Cuban, owner of the Dallas Mavericks

Everyone knows and has heard of a story of jobs being moved overseas. The industrial rust belt of America felt this over 10 years ago. No better time than now to take your own future in your hands.

Dejobbing of America automation is the wave of the future needing less and less people to operate and run manufacturing jobs and office/white collar jobs. The industrial belt of America has been hit hard since the 1980s and truly never recovered. Do not be a person unwilling to attend other skills or be flexible on your career journey.

Chapter 10

Less workers needed

Between **90 and 95 million low-skill workers -- or 2.6 percent of the global workforce -- will not be needed by employers by 2020 and will be vulnerable to permanent joblessness**, according to a report released Thursday by the McKinsey Global Institute. Meanwhile, employers around the world will need nearly 45 million more medium-skill workers (with secondary school and vocational training) and 38 to 40 million more high-skill workers (with a college education) than will be available, according to the study. (http://www.huffingtonpost.com/2012/06/19/unskilled-workers-2020-mckinsey-global-institute-study_n_1609767.html)

Imagine that? 90-95 million people going to be jobless without NEW, HIGHER SKILLS. Now I do believe there will always be service jobs cooking, cleaning, cutting grass and car repair. This time you will have to be the owner of that service company to make a living. You will have to depend on your hustle skills or hiring a marketer/full time promotion person to get the business and income you need.

Older workers staying longer many baby boomers should be kicking their heels up and enjoying retirement or part time work right? Wrong. Millions of baby boomers in their 50s have less than 10,000 dollars saved for retirement. That's sad. If I was 50 with this issue I would immediately get a paid off car and keep it for the next 10 years. On top of that I would be investing in monthly dividend stocks or cheap real estate on the edges of town.

80% of jobs will be service related in the future. People hate service I do not know why, the more people you serve the more you make. Chick fila makes the millions or billions because of the great service. People love hearing "my pleasure" and "have a great day". It also helps to have great chicken. Zig ziglar say if you help enough people get what they want you will get what you want.

Joseph Poole will make more than $100,000 in wages and overtime by the end of the year. The 21-year-old works in what looks like NASA's mission control, monitoring the manufacturing process at Chevron Phillips petrochemical plant in

Houston. Poole didn't get the job with the engineering degree he originally considered. Instead, Poole landed it with a two-year course at a local community college.

"The potential to make just as much money as an engineer, but for half the cost of the education, was here," Poole says. "Just seeing firsthand how things are made is something I really enjoy doing."

By 2017, an estimated 2.5 million new, middle-skill jobs like Poole's are expected to be added to the workforce, accounting for nearly 40% of all job growth, according to a USA TODAY analysis of local data from Economic Modeling Specialists Intl. and CareerBuilder. (http://www.usatoday.com/story/news/nation/2014/09/30/job-economy-middle-skill-growth-wage-blue-collar/14797413/)

So on one hand we are losing jobs, but we are getting more skilled intensive jobs.

Chapter 11

Why it's easier than ever to start a company

"Opportunity is missed by most people because it is dressed in overalls and looks like work." --Thomas Edison, inventor

9 year old creates Sweet bee lemonade in Austin

When I was just four, my family encouraged me to make a product for a Children's business competition (the Acton Children's Business Fair) and

Austin Lemonade Day. So I put on my thinking cap. I thought about some ideas. While I was thinking, two big events happened.

I got stung by a bee. Twice.

Then my Great Granny Helen, who lives in Cameron, South Carolina, sent my family a 1940's cookbook, which included her special recipe for Flaxseed Lemonade.

I didn't enjoy the bee stings at all. They scared me. But then something strange happened. I became fascinated with bees. I learned all about what they do for me and our ecosystem. So then I thought, what if I make something that helps honeybees and uses my Great Granny Helen's recipe?

That's how BeeSweet Lemonade was born. It comes from my Great Granny Helen's flaxseed recipe and my new love for bees. So that's why we sweeten it with local honey. And today my little idea continues to grow.

It was a sweet success from the start. Year-after-year, Mikaila, sells-out of her BeeSweet Lemonade at youth entrepreneurial events while donating a percentage of the profits from the sale of her lemonade to local and international organizations fighting hard to save the honeybees. That is why she touts: Buy a Bottle...Save a Bee.

Now at age 10, when not at her lemonade stand telling all the digestive benefits of flaxseed, you can find Mikaila leading workshops on how to save the honeybees, and participating in social entrepreneurship panels. Mikaila launched her own Facebook page, where visitors can 'Like' interesting facts about bees, honey and BeeSweet Lemonade.

Today, the award-winning BeeSweet Lemonade is buzzing off the shelves of Whole Foods Market, the world's leader in natural and organic foods, and available at a growing number of restaurants, food trailers and natural food delivery companies.

Mikaila Ulmer: A social entrepreneur, bee ambassador, educator and student. (http://beesweetlemonade.com/pages/about-us)

5 and 7 Year old Youtube Cooking stars.

YouTube stars are becoming more and more like Hollywood celebrities, with hordes of screaming fans and generous incomes.

But it turns out that they may be making even more money than you think.

AdAge recently published a ranking of the top YouTube stars according to their estimated monthly earnings.

The data was compiled by Outrigger Media, who focused on the top-earning channels in two genres: beauty and style, and food and cooking.

The top earner in the food and cooking genre is a channel called CharlisCraftyKitchen, which features videos of an 8-year-old named Charli sharing baking tips.

According to Outrigger's estimates, Charli's channel generates an average of $127,777 in ad revenue per month. That's taking into account YouTube's cut of revenue. The channel gets an average of 29 million views each month — in March, it had 29,133,270. Charli began making her videos in 2012, when she was 6. Her 5-year-old sister, Ashlee, also plays a role as chief taste tester. The girls have made tutorials for everything from Minnie Mouse Oreo pops to jello popsicles inspired by "Frozen."http://www.entrepreneur.com/article/245205)

7 Louisville Ketucky teens start Tech Company.

7 Louisville teens start Tech Company, the teenagers were taught to code and create websites. This is an amazing feat for teenagers to realize they can create their own company. This is what America is great for, any one of any generation or economic background can start a business with the right skills. In an attempt to stay ahead of the technology curve, a collaboration between the Metro Louisville Department of Economic Growth and Innovation, Greater Louisville Inc, EnterpriseCorp, the Louisville Free Public Library, KentuckianaWorks and local employers was established to create the technology

growth program known as Code Louisville.

The program consists of a series of twelve-week sessions which uses the Treehouse coding program to train future software developers. According to the Code Louisville website, between 2010 and 2020, Louisville is projected to have a net increase of nearly 2000 new programmer and software developer jobs. In 2015, Code Louisville decided to expand its training program to include high school students from Louisville's predominately black Russell Neighborhood, so it created a pilot program called Code Louisville After School. Classes for the the program would be held at the city owned learning center in the Russell Neighborhood known as The Beech. (http://urbanmaxx.com/2015/07/02/7-louisville-teenagers-create-a-tech-company-building-websites/)

Durham high school students start bank

From WUNC.org article:

Financial literacy is a growing part of the K-through-12 curriculum across the state. But Hillside High School in Durham has taken the charge to the next level and opened a functioning bank branch at the school.

Organizers say that students, staff, and families will be able to open accounts, as well as deposit funds to checking and savings accounts right at the Hillside branch. The program also provides internships and serves as a hands-on learning center for students to gain banking skills.

One of the first people to open an account at Hillside's Student Bank Training Center was New

Tech director Tounya Wright.

"I'm just loving this, I'm excited about it, it's going to be so convenient to be able to have this money here on campus," said White.

There is a staff that's been hired for this branch, there is a manager and service representatives and so they facilitate everything. -Jessica Valentine

The bank is an official branch of Woodforest National Bank, based in Texas, and is a partnership with Hillside's Business and Finance Academy.

Woodforest National is a community bank with more than 80 outlets across North Carolina. Senior Vice President Jessica Valentine says this is their first time opening a high school branch.

(http://wunc.org/post/durham-ncs-hillside-high-school-first-open-bank)

Musician gets $75,000 a month from online website

From Business insider article:

In 2009, just after Graham Cochrane moved to Florida with his wife and newborn daughter, the startup he worked for went under and he lost his job. "I have never been entrepreneurial," he says. "I was a scaredy cat. I wanted a stable job to pay my bills and not have debt."

In fact, he had purchased Tim Ferriss' classic "The 4-Hour Workweek," read it, and returned it because he thought the book's ideas were so far from his reality he couldn't use a single one.

But with savings dwindling, he turned to the passion-project-slash-side-job he had been pursuing through his 20s: freelance recording and sound mixing. He had been bringing in an extra $1,000-$2,000 a month, and while he and his wife, a photographer, had some savings, he hoped he could ramp up his freelancing enough to replace his $50,000 annual income.

Along with his side job, the now 32-year-old had started a casual blog to provide answers to the steady stream of emails he had been getting from friends and acquaintances asking technical questions. In January of 2010, he rebranded that blog The Recording Revolution, and he remembers it made hardly any money at all in its first two years. Today, nearly six years after he made it his primary focus, the site earns between $35,000 and $75,000 a month.

Aside from the free content he's always offered,

Cochrane added in-depth video courses on different aspects of sound recording and mixing that cost between $39 and $897, and a monthly membership for $27 a month that provides access to supplementary content. He estimates between 6,000 and 7,000 people have taken his courses so far. "It's a weird phenomenon," he says. "Because I was a musician, I expected never to make any money."

Read more:

http://www.businessinsider.com/graham-cochrane-recording-revolution-2015-6#ixzz3iIny5M2y

Making $50,000 a year while traveling

Made $50,000 a year while traveling all year long. Within six months I had 500 readers a day. By the end of the first year I had 3,000 daily readers, and I was making $1,000 a month from advertising and selling affiliate products. Best of all, I loved sharing stories on a blog. It gave me the ingredient I was missing — creative expression. I had finally found the right business for me. In my second year of blogging I made two very important decisions that would eventually lead me to become a blogging millionaire.1. I started an email newsletter to go with my blog.2. I decided to sell my own teaching products. Using my blog and my email list I launched a course called BlogMastermind.com in 2007 to teach people how to start a blog that makes money. Just under 400 people enrolled for $27 per month and I found myself earning $15,000 a month in revenue. As part of the launch, I gave away a free report called the Blog Profits Blueprint, which has been downloaded over 100,000 times. Later, I increased the price to $49 a month, then $97 a month or a $497 one-time fee, after turning it into a six-month course rather than an ongoing membership. Read more: http://www.businessinsider.com/yaro-starak-entrepreneurs-journey-2015-6#ixzz3gbKL8jA8 (http://www.businessinsider.com/yaro-starak-entrepreneurs-journey-2015-6)

Sean ogle

Ever come back from vacation and go, why am I working so many hours at this job? Well that's Sean ogle. He went to visit friend in Hawaii, wanted more time off or to work remotely. His company fired him for not taking his work seriously.

Excerpt from his blog :

I graduated from Oregon State University in 2007 with a degree in finance. I had a fantastic time at my 4 years in school, but I can't help but feel it didn't prepare me with the real life, tangible skills that I needed to be successful after graduation.

This led me to a job as a financial analyst that I quickly found wasn't for me. Working 50 hours a week, wearing a suit and tie, and not having any of the flexibility to do the things that excited me grew old *really* quickly.

Sound familiar?

I started Location 180 in May 2009 to hold myself accountable for doing all of the cool stuff in life I've always talked about. I published my bucket list, and have been working through it ever since. So far I'm doing pretty good, I've lived on a tropical island, built a business, ran a marathon, and climbed a mountain, among other things.

Somehow I've gotta support the cool lifestyle though. In January 2010 I headed to Thailand to work with the Tropical MBA which has evolved into a full time business doing SEO, consulting, affiliate marketing, and anything else that seems interesting to me.

Once I moved to Thailand it didn't take long before I realized just how attainable my dream lifestyle was, merely by utilizing the power of the internet. Within a few months I was making enough to support my lifestyle and these days I have the flexibility to pretty much do whatever I want, whenever I want.

Location 180 and it's sister site Location Rebel are all about helping you to achieve the same lifestyle. One where you can do more of the stuff that makes you happy, and help others in the process.

- See more at:

http://www.seanogle.com/about#sthash.EolbNGtW.dpuf

19 Year old earned 100,000 on etsy

LeiLei Secor is a 19-year old University of Virginia student. She's spending her summer working for her local congressman near Albany, New York where she grew up. She's also the owner of Designed by Lei, an Etsy store that has made more than $100,000 in three years. She's using that money to pay her way through college. (http://www.theblackhomeschool.com/2015/06/25/how-a-19-year-old-made-over-100000-on-etsy-to-pay-for-college/)

Imagine the confidence this college student has knowing she help paid for college. The additional confidence of knowing she can start a business and make $100,000 dollars once she can do it again. Marketing and Time Management was the big lessons she learned from this experience.

17 Year old earns 1.7 million from youtube.

17 year old earns 1.7 million in sales from Youtube blog wild daisy forever on Youtube. Her father gave her money to buy things from alabalia/china and then resell and build up designs and clothing/fashion ideas. The best part of her story is her father giving her $250 to start her business and she has been profitable ever since.

Imagine as a parent how you can encourage your kids entrepreneur dreams and aspirations.

Over 10 bloggers making 100k a year

Mostly fashion related blogs some travel, lifestyle, and photography make headway. Taken from the richest.com article "In today's digital age, it's become more and more common to hear about people giving up their 9-5 desk jobs in favour of pursuing their freelance dreams. Sure, sometimes it doesn't work out and they crash and burn before quickly returning to a steady source of income – but sometimes it does. In a big way. It's not unheard of to learn of bloggers making over six figures per year off of the content they post. The Internet is a huge place and there's a demographic for all sorts of content; whether you're writing about health, travel, fashion, food or photography. Many of the most successful bloggers have zeroed in on a specific niche and have become pioneers in their chosen fields as a result.

They know that there's an entire world hungry for information out there and that their websites provide the instant, gratifying eye candy or reading material that their demographic craves.

The best bloggers have made it to where they are by consistently posting new content and constantly finding creative ways to communicate with their target market. After building up an audience, their revenue comes from ad sales on their sites or partnerships with like-minded brands and companies. $5,000 to $10,000 is the standard fee paid out to top fashion and lifestyle bloggers nowadays to make an appearance at an event and endorse it to their endless followers. From there, they are often given the opportunity to collaborate with companies by producing content for them or designing products for them to sell. As if that wasn't enough to think about, many bloggers have vocalized the need to be selective when it comes to partnerships in order to keep their images on brand. We've compiled a list of ten of the most successful ones who make over $100,000 per year and have made a full-time job out of pursuing their passions." (http://www.therichest.com/business/salary/10-bloggers-who-make-over-100k-per-year/?view=all)

Largest Marketplace for doll clothing patterns

Cinnamon and Jason Miles We run the Internet's largest marketplace for doll clothing patterns at Pixie Faire, featuring more than 50 indie designers, as well as online training courses on design, sewing, pattern-making, and craft business. We also sell our doll clothing and patterns under our brand Liberty Jane Clothing. How much revenue are you currently generating per month? Our conservative estimate for total revenue for this year is $600,000 US, which is $50,000 a month, although there is some seasonality. (http://www.shopify.com/blog/17587420-how-one-couple-is-making-600-000-per-year-selling-digital-products?utm_source=exacttarget&utm_medium=email&utm_campaign=digest&email-link=1)

Five Figure Frankstein Pumpkin Farmer

Man creates Frankstein molds for his 40 acre farm in California so the pumpkins grow into the shape of Frankstein head. It's amazing he sells them for $75-$100 apiece. Imagine 3000 pumpkins x 100= $300,000 off one harvest.

(http://www.nytimes.com/2014/10/13/us/its-alive-and-it-grows-into-a-jack-o-lantern.html?_r=1)

This is why I am so hard on people in rural areas with land all around them yet not working on it to produce any saleable items. Mini farming can be tiring but we are encountering a generation of people stuck to their TV and computers instead of using practical ideas to become free.

Authors still making money

Chandler Bolt comes out of Charleston South Carolina and wrote 4 best sellers and created a company teaching other authors how to publish and launch their books. Great part he quit college and is just 21 years old. Here is a excerpt from the article.

With his scholarships and paying instate tuition, it would have cost him $7,000 plus living expenses to finish the next two years of school. "I looked at it like opportunity cost," he says. "Not what would it cost to finish, but what could I accomplish in this time? What could I be doing? How is school limiting me?"

While interning with a work-experience company called Student Painters and attending classes, Bolt coauthored and self-published a book on time management in November 2013 called "The Productive Person," based on the insights he had gleaned from working and studying in his teens.

The first month after publishing, it brought in nearly $7,000 that he split with his business partner James Roper, now 26, whom Bolt met through Student Painters. The book continued to steadily earn between $2,000 and $5,000 a month.

He delayed leaving school until after getting the chance to study abroad in Austria during his junior year, where one day a friend asked whether the book he had written was making any money.

"Well," he answered, "we were snowboarding all day yesterday, and I made $400."

(http://www.businessinsider.com/chandler-bolt-self-publishing-school-2015)

Chapter 12

Driver contracts

Now more than ever all you need is a car to get you around to making 100,000 a year. You can create many companies from car related services. The trucking industry is still short on drivers. Well not everyone wants to travel around the country on a semi, but you can your personal driving economy with your car. From delivery routes for UPS, FedEx, Bread companies, part time carrier contracts, there are many opportunities in driving if you have a modern car or spacious truck. The opportunities are endless, and only limited by your imagination.

Uber worth 50 billion dollars, operating in 260 cities

in the world.

Uber driver made 252,000 a year.

Had a jewelry company made $3,000 a month from Uber, and $18,000 a month in jewelry sales. Had jewelry placed in his car and if people started conversation he told them about it. He had a mobile billboard that was basically in front of you.

In the same vein UBER, Lyft, ride share, and side car all provide rides via apps on your phone.

Lyft

Ride share

Side car

Lyft is partnering with Starbucks to give employees free rides to and from work. It's a great partnership. Lyft is trying to fill the voids and other ideas left on the table by UBER. Read more at

(http://www.forbes.com/sites/erikamorphy/2015/07/26/lyft-makes-starbucks-an-offer-it-couldnt-refuse/)

Relay Rides

Relay rides you are able to rent your car out daily for $23-$150 dollars or more a day. I know people with an older Honda or Mazda they drove in college, or an extra car at their house just sitting there getting no use.

Urban mail routes

You every lived in a small town, or a smaller city. How do the country folk get their mail? The United States said instead of paying for several workers to go out in the sticks to deliver mail to distance routes them sale off government contracts for the job. It's not uncommon for a rural mail route to make you $100,000 a year. The best part so many tax write offs, and not every house will get mail every day.

Bread truck delivery routes

Have a commercial van or larger size truck? Well you could be a bread delivery driver, its several routes for sale on different websites. I love buy biz sell.com it offers opportunity to sell operating businesses, fedex/UPS routes and bread routes. Independent contractors operate heavily in these markets.

Chapter 13

Service companies

The service industry is one of the easiest and best industry to be in. You can pick up your business in a few hours. Literally fill out doing business as form, business bank account, some business cards or flyers, then head out.

Most popular

Landscaping, home repairs, windshield repair, and Business to business operations, a massive and lucrative field. There are so many things and services small businesses need. One problem they have no time to fix them. That is where temp workers, contract workers, and other small businesses specializing in accounting or other services come in.

Personal assistant Services Company is another instant start today company. Marketing your services to the wealthy or business owner looking for more time.

Chapter 14

Administrative

Companies want to transfer over to less responsibilities for keeping workers. Less insurance, less taxes and less costs to the company. How can they do this effectively? They hire out temp workers. Independent contractors fill the voids that temp workers cannot. People can work independent of managers or micro managing.

Some sites to check out for opportunities.

Freelancer.com

We work spaces

Task rabbit

Temp working companies liberty group

Chapter 15

Online business

Shopify

Shopify is a complete ecommerce solution that allows you to set up an online store to sell your goods. It lets you organize your products, customize your storefront, accept credit card payments, track and respond to orders — all with a few clicks of the mouse.

Shopify's Build A Business Competition is bigger than ever. Shopify is giving away more than $500,000 in cash, prizes and mentorship in its fourth annual competition. Contestants create a store and

try to sell the most in their category for a chance to win $50,000 and a VIP trip to NYC to meet their mentor.
(http://www.huffingtonpost.com/shopify/how-i-doubled-my-sales-us_b_4440049.html)

Shopify success story

Dodo case

DODOcase – A San Francisco startup looking to preserve historic book binding techniques – needed an ecommerce solution to begin selling their famous iPad cases.

The fact that Shopify's platform had everything they were looking for was enhanced by the opportunity to enter Shopify's first ever Build A Business competition, where they could win $100,000. Little did they know that not only would they win the competition, but they would bring in $3 million in sales during their first year on Shopify. (https://www.shopify.com/plus/customers/dodocase)

Music/Youtube Fame into Profits.

Scott Bradlee Post Modern Jukebox Youtube. Excerpt from Wikipedia Does the greatest job of explaining the phenomena that is Post Modern Juke Box.

Article on Scott Bradlee:

Scott is a piano player and formed Postmodern Jukebox. Bradlee lived his earliest years in the Long Island community of Nesconset, New York. He moved at age four and grew up in the Pattenburg section of Union Township, Hunterdon County, New Jersey where he fell in love with jazz at the age of 12 after hearing George Gershwin's *Rhapsody in Blue* for the first time.

Bradlee became a successful performer in the New York jazz scene,[5] and served as music director for an interactive, off-Broadway theater experience called *Sleep No More.*

In looking for creative inspiration, Bradlee began reworking popular music as an exercise. In 2009, he released "Hello My Ragtime '80s", which incorporated ragtime-style piano into popular music from the 1980s. After playing and experimenting on stage at his regular gig at Robert Restaurant, he released the compilation *Mashups by Candlelight.* Bradlee gained popularity in 2012 with *A Motown Tribute to Nickelback*, a collaboration with local musicians which arranged Nickelback's songs in the style of 1960s style R&B music. In 2013, Bradlee began to work more seriously on forming Postmodern Jukebox, a rotating group of musicians producing covers of pop songs in the styles of jazz, ragtime, and swing. The group burst onto the public radar with their doo-wop cover of Miley Cyrus' "We Can't Stop", featuring vocal group The Tee-Tones. As the viral surge grew, Bradlee was interviewed by news outlets such as NPR[6] and also performed live on *Good Morning America* and Fuse.[7] The group visited *Cosmopolitan Magazine's* New York office for a year-end review of their work and popular songs from the year.[8]

Several artists have publicly noted their appreciation for the group's work. Among the group's prominent guest musicians are Dave Koz, who collaborated with them in a jazz covers of "Careless Whisper" and the *Game of Thrones* theme music, and Niia, who joined them for a "space jazz" version of "The End of the World". Postmodern Jukebox's October 2013 collaboration with Puddles Pity Party on a cover of Lorde's "Royals" generated particularly strong interest; as of September 2014, this video remained the second most popular on Bradlee's YouTube channel with over 8.7 million hits.[9]

In 2013, Bradlee found interest from the video game industry, gaining a composer credit for 2K Games' *BioShock Infinite* soundtrack, which features four of his stylized arrangements: a piano cover of Tears for Fears' "Everybody Wants to Rule the World" (piano and vocals), a jazzy ragtime cover of Gloria Jones' "Tainted Love" (arrangement, piano), and covers of R.E.M.'s "Shiny Happy People" (arrangement and piano) and "After You've Gone" (arrangement, piano).

In early September 2014, Bradlee uploaded a 1940s jazz interpretation of "All About That Bass" called "All

About That (Upright) Bass", featuring Kate Davissinging solo while playing double bass, with Bradlee on piano and Dave Tedeschi on drums. The video received 8 million hits in three months.[13][14] Also in 2014, Bradlee's YouTube Channel "Postmodern Jukebox" was listed as #42 on *NewMediaRockstars'* "Top 100 Channels".[15] In late 2014 to 2015, his band was to tour America and Europe. (https://en.wikipedia.org/wiki/Scott_Bradlee)

Using Youtube allow Scott Bradlee the opportunity to tour the world and it started with free video on YouTube and interaction with fans and subscribers. It's important to monetize YouTube for your benefit not just ad words, but projects, events, tours and CDs/digital downloads if you are artist.

Musicians creating own company

Ryan Leslie Music and Online Mogul while working as a producer, Leslie went on to create Next Selection Lifestyle Group, his music-media company he founded with online marketing partner Rasheed Richmond. Ryan signed his first artist, Cassie in 2005. Under Ryan's guidance, Cassie went on to become one of the fastest rising R&B acts that year. Her breakout smash "Me & U" (written and produced by Leslie) spent 20 weeks on the Top 40 and went on to reach number three on the Billboard Hot 100, selling over a million digital units. "Me & U" also went on to become one of the biggest records in the history of Atlantic Records.[16]

Ryan posts an interactive daily video blog, where he

gives viewers a taste of what daily life is like in the music business. Industry parties, TV appearances, and hanging out with beautiful women—it's there for all to see. "Blogging is something that allows us to document life," Leslie said. "When you look at a lot of successful films, books, and a lot of them relate to the experiences of others," and the video blog is a way for him to connect with the masses. "There have been other video blogs, but this one's a first of its kind from a music standpoint," he said [17] "It's a huge commitment," he said of the video blog. "It takes six, seven hours a day to produce a video blog." [17] In anticipation for the release of Les Is More, Leslie releases a new music video from his album for every video that reaches one million hits on his website [8]. Recently, Ryan signed Krys Ivory as his newest act under Next Selection.[18] He also signed YouTube star Mia Rose.

Disruptive Multimedia [edit]

In August 2013, Leslie released his fourth studio album, Black Mozart, through his #Renegades music club.[19] In subsequent months, musicians such as 50 Cent, Raphael Saadiq, and Talib Kweli would use the underlying technology to launch their respective upcoming studio albums and power their own music membership clubs.[20] Kweli spoke about the experience in an interview, "The first thing that appeals to me is the direct contact with the fans and the fact that I receive their e-mails...The second thing is the fact that the money comes directly to me when you buy the album from me. It goes directly to my account. There is nobody taking their cut."[21] Ryan Leslie also teaches other artists how to create an online business and go touring around the world via their cell phone. It's amazing how you do not need a record label anymore. It's about how business minded are you.

Guy singing in Apple store

Article from New York Post :

A broke Brooklyn rapper spent four months recording an entire album using the display computers at the Apple Store in Soho.

Prince Harvey, 25, spent every weekday singing, humming and rapping into a floor computer at the Prince Street location.

Harvey said he pulled off the coup with the help of two particularly understanding store employees, and a friend who came in to record backup vocals.

"It wasn't my plan to record this at the Apple Store. First, my computer died. Then my external [hard drive] died," Harvey told the Daily Beast. "New York is expensive. I couldn't just buy another laptop. I just thought, 'I'm going to die before anyone knows I'm hot.'"

Modal Trigger

Harvey said he dodged the store's end-of-day policy of wiping its display computers' memory by hiding files in the devices' trash.

He said he also relied on e-mail and a thumb drive to store his work.

It usually did the trick.

But "one time, there was a fire drill, and I was trying to save my work, and this lady came over and disconnected the thumb drive while it was saving," he lamented.

Harvey said that while he's grateful to the pair of Apple workers who looked the other way while he belted out his tunes, he wants to keep them anonymous. (http://nypost.com/2015/07/07/broke-rapper-records-entire-album-at-apple-store/)

Chapter 16

EBooks, programs

Many bloggers are cashing in on kindle book publishing. Such as project life majesty? **Stefan Pylarinos** is making thousands of dollars a month from kindle ebooks. Many Americans and Europeans are looking for ways to educate themselves quickly and use kindle and tablets to download books to read.

There are so many book ideas or extended blog ideas that can be 30-60 page ebooks for people to quickly learn a skill and move forward. Information is power is the old saying. Truly information plus action is the real power a person can display.

Marketing Zen Group

Article on Shama Hyder:

Marketing Zen group she created after getting multiple degrees and could not find a job. SHAMA HYDER GRADUATED AT THE TOP OF HER CLASS — TWICE — AND STILL FACED 18 JOB REJECTIONS AFTER RECEIVING HER MASTER'S. THE PROBLEM? SHE WANTED TO GO INTO SOCIAL MEDIA MARKETING BEFORE SOCIAL MEDIA HAD BECOME AN INTEGRAL PART OF EVERY BUSINESS — NO ONE REALLY KNEW WHAT IT WAS YET. SO SHE STARTED TO BLOG, WHICH TURNED INTO THE BESTSELLING BOOK The Zen of Social Media Marketing AND CLIENTS CAME KNOCKING ON HER DOOR ASKING HER

TO HELP THEM WITH THEIR ONLINE PRESENCE.

TODAY, HYDER IS THE CEO OF MARKETING ZEN GROUP, AND SHE'S BEEN RECOGNIZED AS A LEADER IN DIGITAL MARKETING TRENDS BY Business Week, Forbes, Bloomberg, Entrepreneur, AND Fast Company. SHE HAS TRAVELED THE WORLD AS A KEYNOTE SPEAKER — LEADING DISCUSSIONS EVERYWHERE FROM THE WHITE HOUSE TO CAIRO — AND IS A REGULAR CONTRIBUTOR TO FOX BUSINESS, CBS, AND MSNBC.

HYDER, 29, REFLECTS ON THE VALUE OF A BICULTURAL EDUCATION, THE MOTIVATION THAT COMES FROM REJECTION, AND THE JOYS OF A VIRTUAL OFFICE.

(http://www.cosmopolitan.com/career/interviews/a

38342/get-that-life-shama-hyder-marketing-zen-group/)

Chapter 17

Consulting

Everyone needs a coach. It doesn't matter whether you're a basketball player, a tennis player, a gymnast or a bridge player.
Bill gates

Consulting is a multimillion dollar industry with great opportunity for those with skills to offer and fix other companies. Consulting can be simple or complex as the client needs it to be. I have found 100s of different niches online.

Online consulting a popular trending type of consulting where online life coaches or business startup coaches are helping millions gain skills and knowledge to grow or start companies.

Online mentorship is different from coaching that is part time or short term. Mentorship will along a person to have someone walk alongside them for a year to two years of their journey. It's important to have positive reinforcing individuals in your life. I think the reason so many entrepreneurs fail is lack of capital and lack of belief.

Many of your friends and family will not understand your desire to leave a "safe and secure" job. It's not their nature. God gave you the gifts and talents you have, do not waste them. The worst thing is seeing someone about 40-60 living a life of regret.

Chapter 18

Honey

Bees are dying off

From the article on CNBC:

Widespread deaths among bees, known as Colony Collapse Disorder, were first reported about a decade ago, but the problem has not diminished and may have been especially bad recently.

Beekeepers across the United States lost roughly 40 percent of their colonies from April 2014 to April 2015, according to an annual survey conducted by the Bee Informed Partnership and Apiary Inspectors of America, with funding from the U.S. Department of Agriculture.

That's the second highest percentage loss since researchers began counting summer and winter season losses five years ago.

The group found that large numbers of bees are dying during the summer months, when conditions should be more favorable. One in 4 colonies is now dying during summer, which was unheard of several years ago, according to the results.

The total number of bee colonies in the United States declined from 6 million during the 1940s to 2.5 million about 10 years ago, but it has remained relatively stable since then. The most recent numbers place the total estimate at 2.74 million.

Beekeepers expect to lose a small number of colonies every year, especially in winter months when food supplies are scarce. Beekeepers can replace those losses by splitting a healthy colony of bees in

half and buying a new queen to start a new colony.
(http://www.cnbc.com/2015/05/14/honeybees-are-dying-and-us-fruit-and-nut-crops-may-suffer.html)

Round rock honey

Honey sales last year in the Austin area totaled $380,000, and this year the company is on track to pull in $1.5 million between Dallas-area farmer's markets sales and Austin-area sales, he says. (http://www.bizjournals.com/austin/stories/2008/06/02/story5.html)

Round rock honey business includes HEB and Whole Foods store contracts, local restaurant contracts, and teaching about honey bees. They offer Groupon deals to spending 1 to 3 hours with the honey bees and learning the honey business and process.

Starting a honey company

You can buy a hive for about $290 on craigslist or a local bee/honey business. Your business can be broken down in many ways. You can carry bees from farm to farm. Its popular for local to large size farmers to use bees to improve their agriculture gains, as well it's cheaper to allow a bee specialist to bring bees then start the process themselves.

Selling honey at farmers markets, online and getting grocery store contracts. You do not need much land for this operation and could be a great side income in the summer. A honey business could be great for teenagers, or college students with some summer free time.

Chapter 19

Coffee

"As long as there was coffee in the world, how bad could things be?"

— Cassandra Clare, *City of Ashes*

"Adventure in life is good; consistency in coffee even better."

— Justina Chen, *North of Beautiful*

"There were some problems only coffee and ice cream could fix."

— Amal El-Mohtar, *Steam-Powered: Lesbian Steampunk Stories*

"Coffee and chocolate—the inventor of mocha should be sainted."

— Cherise Sinclair, *Hour of the Lion*

100 billion dollar industry

There's no shame in coming in second place to oil. Coffee is worth over $100 billion worldwide.

That puts it ahead of commodities like natural gas, gold, brent oil, sugar and corn.

Read more: http://www.businessinsider.com/facts-about-the-coffee-industry-2011-11#ixzz3iqNPOmdk

Coffee is grown in over 50 countries in Asia, Africa, South America, Central America and the Caribbean. And 67 percent of the world's coffee is grown in the Americas alone.

Read more: http://www.businessinsider.com/facts-about-the-coffee-industry-2011-11#ixzz3iqNjOLt2

It's an understatement to say America loves it coffee. It loves it so much there is a Starbucks offering 5 dollar coffee on multiple corners of a city and additional independent coffee shops scattered across college towns.

Kickstarter coffee success stories

There are thousands of kickstarter coffee shop or coffee related products. The opportunity to draw sales and a following in your local city can be created through kickstarter. Look for some successful companies and see if you can create a story you want to share.

Sunset Coffee Shop

Coffee shop still a great opportunity depending on the city. I would google hipster cities and locations. Living in Austin Texas the city cannot get enough of them. I have visited several on one day looking for somewhere to sit down and do quick work. Most are completely packed.

I owned a coffee shop and learned a little too late the power of the internet. I could have built two platforms for my business. My business was located in Fayetteville North Carolina across from a college campus. I had steady business, but then city decided to tear up the road making it unsafe for students to travel and cars to turn off business road.

I strongly suggest if owning a coffee shop has been your dream to invest in an online business, sell bags on amazon fulfillment, and roast your own beans. I recommend you own the building or structure the rent to be really low for several years. These different angles of business I learned way too late.

Chapter 20

Body butters

Kim Kardashian has made many small body butter companies overnight sell outs when she would post their product to her twitter and Instagram pages. I am not saying hope for a celebrity to make you famous, but there is a niche out there for you. Many people are looking for safer alternatives for soap, lotions and face wash products.

Instagram, Pinterest and blogs are covered in ways to create and sell body butters. I would come up with a creative niche and make yourself know as an expert or top salesperson in your area. I would do countless youtube videos, facebook videos, facebook ads. Work on getting your product put in stores, barbershops and hair salons. Know your skill level if you lack time and salesperson qualities then focus on building an online following.

Chapter 21

Natural hair products/Hair products

Perm industry loses 80+ millions of dollars

The Black haircare industry is grossly underestimated, and knowingly so. Market research firm Mintel estimated the size of the 2012 market at $684 million, with a projection of $761 million by 2017. But Mintel also wisely notes: What's missing from these figures are general market brands, weaves, extensions, wigs, independent beauty supply stores, distributors, e-commerce, styling tools

and appliances. If all of those things were to be taken into consideration, the $684 million in expenditures could reach a whopping half trillion dollars.
Half trillion, as is in $500 billion. That's more than double Greece's Gross Domestic Product.
Hair is an important aspect of Black female culture, so it's unsurprising that we potentially spend that much money on our hair. *Good Hair*, the 2009 documentary by comedian Chris Rock, shined a spotlight on the business of black hair, particularly our use of relaxers and weaves and the sources of the extensions so many women sew into their hair. Since Rock's reveal of the industry, much has and hasn't changed in the world of Black hair.

http://www.huffingtonpost.com/antonia-opiah/the-changing-business-of-_b_4650819.html

Opportunity abounds for people wanting to get their hands on a huge industry.

Sisters success stories

Miss Jessie has become a MULTIMILLION dollar company due to the focus on the rising tide of natural hair in the African American community in United States. The sister Miko Branch wrote a book of their experience in starting the company. Excerpt from amazon book:

Miss Jessie's is a memoir and business guide rich with inspirational life lessons and unique business advice from Miko Branch, the Chief Executive Officer of the dynamic Miss Jessie's — the company that revolutionized the hair care industry.

When Miko and her sister, Titi, were children, their grandmother, Miss Jessie, taught them independence and showed them the value of being "do it yourself" women, all while whipping up homemade hair concoctions at her kitchen table. As co-founders of

Miss Jessie's, Miko reveals how she and Titi applied those lessons to create a successful business from scratch.

A family memoir with a wealth of practical business advice and handy hair tips, told in Miko's funny and relatable voice, *Miss Jessie's* is her remarkable story — from her childhood learning independence as a latchkey kid in Jamaica, Queens, to building a highly regarded company with her sister in their shared home salon in Bedford-Stuyvesant, Brooklyn. Miko reflects on her hard-won insights working for her autocratic, iron-fisted father, and how the self-sufficiency she learned in childhood helped her blossom as a single mother with bills to pay, a child to raise, and a dream to pursue. She speaks honestly of her mistakes and successes, and of her role as an industry leader, negotiating multi-million dollar deals while at the same time restoring the self-esteem of natural and curly haired women.

Charming and enlightening, chock full of entertaining stories and invaluable instruction that can be applied to any business, and illustrated with 16 pages of photos, Miss Jessie's confirms that with effort the American Dream is possible.

(http://www.amazon.com/Miss-Jessies-Creating-Successful-Scratch-Naturally/dp/0062329189)

Brazil has a bunch of brand new millionaires in hair industry

Brazil never experienced a civil rights movement. The northern part of the whole country is about 80-90% black or look African. There were a high number of slaves delivered to northern Brazil. The current trends in hair and clothing is AINT European. With the turn against, straightening, perms going to afros, curly hair the hair industry is booming. Multiple startups of natural hair care product companies are making millions in a changing nation.

Men natural hair care

Men in large numbers are growing long beards and in general caring about hair care products to fit individualized needs. This has open up the flood gates for men products and millions of dollars.

Bevel, an African American hair care company for men was offered 500 million dollars by Bic and the owner turned it down to keep owning his company. Tristen Walker knew there was a better way to shave for me with curly hair. (http://thegrio.com/2014/02/07/new-startup-bevel-wants-to-rid-black-men-of-bad-haircare/#54296657)

Organic anything

People will pay a premier for organic products. Look at the success of Whole Foods and chipotle. These companies are Uber level successful.

Documentary like Food Inc and other Monsato related documentaries have awakened the American People. Countries all around the world are striving for more direct from the land food experiences.

From farmers shipping direct to the door deliveries to restaurants specializing in local food, organic is in. City restaurants who do Farm to table are becoming extremely popular. Cooking what's in season, local and fresh are bringing in the big bucks.

From organic house cleaners that can help

alleviate your children's sensitive skin to possible pets allergies. People want ways to reduce the level of chemicals, toxins and potential cancer causing products on the market.

Jessica Alba is an actress with a billionaire company owner who started a company about organic baby products because she was concerned about her baby products she was using.

Vitamins

You can start a vitamin company today all the chemical and powders are available to wholesalers. You can buy pill capsules and all ingredients on line. Once they get to your door, you mix the ingredients and BOOM you are vitamin creator.

Industry exploding for body builders

Internet stars and body builders get offers to be spokesman for different products. For the lower level guys they realize they can make their own vitamin company. Protein powder and mixes can be made by just about anyone. This is why it's so important to look who and what is in your vitamins.

Shredz Supplement success

The article excerpt from Forbes.com:

What is the definition of "fitness model?" It was a hotly discussed topic after FORBES published an article on the popular Paige Hathaway, including the Internet sensation as part of a rapidly expanding fitness model classification. The article also raised general awareness for a brand that Paige promotes – SHREDZ – a direct marketing nutritional supplement company. After some investigating it seems that the company Hathaway has partnered with may have an even more interesting story than the fitness model with over 700,000 Instagram followers.

Start with the fact that SHREDZ, founded by current CEO Arvin Lal, earned $90,000 in 2012 (the first year of its operation), $5 million gross revenue in 2013 and already topped $2.7 million through the middle of March in 2014. What makes those numbers more impressive is that Lal and his team have achieved such remarkable revenues without any outside invested capital, only 21 employees (most of them living in-house within the SHREDZ office, which is a converted apartment complex) and purely digital promotion.

Lal has captured the rapidly growing fitness space by going against the grain. He also has a message to those who question whether his endorser, Paige Hathaway is really a fitness model: stop being upset. "Fitness used to be bodybuilding, but today fitness is impacting more people than ever," said Lal to FORBES. "Right now the word 'fitness' has peeked on Google. It's about being healthy and in shape. Who's to say the person on stage has better fitness or body than a person with a million Instagram follows? Paige is probably the largest female fitness model across the world. Marketing and being able to touch people off the stage is more important than being able to touch people on the stage." (http://www.forbes.com/sites/darrenheitner/2014/03/19/instagram-marketing-helped-make-this-multi-million-dollar-nutritional-supplement-company/)

Herbalife millionaires'

Dan Waldron is a 30 year Herbalife veteran. He is affiliated with several businesses that have ties to Herbalife and has the broad smile of a self-made man when he poses for photographs with Michael Johnson and Des Walsh, chief executive and president of the multi-level marketing group.

(http://ftalphaville.ft.com/2014/03/10/1792472/meet-dan-waldron-herbalife-millionaire/)

Usana millionaires

Usana is another vitamin focused direct selling/ Multi- level marketing company that does well in the health care market. Kate Northup the author "money a love story" has a team including her whole family that are high ranking Usana sellers.

Why are vitamins becoming the rage? Cancer, lack of nutrients from food, people wanting to feel better, look better and eat well. People are willing to spend high amounts of money on food, vitamins and gym memberships.

Energy drink

Energy drinks are a billion dollar industry great news you now can get in on the action.

You can create your own energy drink company for about $5,000-10,000 dollars. Companies like power brands, flavor man , monsterbevcorp.com, and vitakem to name a few will send you samples, mix different flavors and have you in business in no time. I think it's much smarter to invest and design your own energy drink brand, then running around selling someone else's. Becoming producers instead of consumers will help you reach next level income.

Amazon and EBay

Amazon is a mammoth in the industry at the moment. From books, clothes, toys, and all the items you can imagine. Some people blame it for the mall closing around America, for the increase in people online shopping.

Amazon millionaires are created every year, if you spend any time on the internet you will see countless books, blogs, and youtube videos of resellers making 6 or 7 figure sales.

Amazon FBA takeover

The key is product diversity. I sell in 10 categories (Music, DVD, toys, video games, books, nutritional supps, grocery, pet supplies, beauty and fitness) and each has their ups and downs. The key is finding products that nobody else is selling that are allowed to be sold here. I am open with hundreds of vendors so I am able to find new products all the time. The key is to walk away once others figure out what you are doing and it gets too competitive.

Do you love to shop and take advantage of great deals? Are you considering starting a side business to bring in extra money?

If so, this opportunity to earn money by shopping for items to resell might be right up your alley: Amazon's **Fulfillment by Amazon** program (FBA). Basically, you find the products you'd like to sell, and

Amazon handles the storage, sales, shipping and customer support.

Ready to learn more? Here's how to know whether FBA is a good option for you — and how to get started.

(http://www.thepennyhoarder.com/make-1000-month-reselling-items-fulfillment-amazon/)

Private label companies

Want to sell yoga mats, yoga pants, fitness gear in general but have your COMPANY logo on it? Well that's what private labeling is all about. It used to be only for the BIG boys, for guys with large company reserves and large product variety. Now you too can create your company and put it on a large amount of made products.

EBay

Not the same as its hay day, it still has sales and eyes attracted to its website. There are ebay millionaires still being made to this day.

Other/craigslist

Craigslist list flipping for money

One of my slow and low series interviewees had not applied for a job since high school. Why because he was purchasing 4 wheelers, scooters and motorcycles off craigslist and turn around fix them a bit and sale them on craigslist again. Now he is further into amazon FBA and daily post office drop offs.

Build your own site

Build your own site and bring traffic to it daily. I read countless blogs, complaints and issues with ebay and amazon accounts being shut down. Imagine getting a bad review and over a 100,000 in value of product being just held hostage at Amazon headquarters. Get more peace of mind by diversifying your product placement and holding.

If you get shut out of a 6 figure business due to PAYPAL holding your money, amazon shutting you down, ebay stopping your business due to a bad review, what will you do? Nothing but wait. Instead building up a diverse websites, or niche websites and learn how to use google ad words or Youtube advertising to bring sales.

Do not believe me? Google and youtube complaints with amazon, ebay and paypal. Do not be held hostage by these websites, but make sure when you do get income you diversify it into multiple streams of passive income.

Chapter 22

Building your personal economy

The average millionaire has 7 streams of income. Most common Farmland, Timber, Rental Income, Precious Metals, Dividend Income, Profit Income, Earned Income, and Insurance.

Think of your personal economy as a table when one leg of the table is out of whack it makes the table wobble. Wobbling is a terrible thing. We want a balance table. The average life span in current jobs for Americans is 2.5 years. Of course you have friends who have been working the same job for 5 or 10 years but keep in mind that is not the normal life span. The

goal here is the buildup streams of income from other sources other than your job. If you really want to live the middle class life style only stocks, bonds, farmland, a side business and rental property is in your future. Only warren buffet lives off stocks alone and it's taken him 50 years to get there.
Think of it as table

You should have stability from multiple streams. There is nothing wrong with having a job, but at least 30% of your income from that job should be used to create other streams of income. It may take years before those streams are full functioning. Insurance is one of those categories if you pay into for 10 years the returns of a cash value policy are great. You will be able to take a loan out against yourself if needed. You can turn around and sell precious metals if there is a crunch. You cannot do these tricks if you never invest in yourself and making your table balance.

I was able to create my own table while working at Lowe's Home Improvement and Papa Johns. Lowe's Home Improvement matched me 6% of my income and I used my papa johns money to invest in lending club, monthly dividend stocks and fund my online business idea. It worked great, until my car had issues and I had to borrow against it. The average life span at a one job is now 2.5 years. Now more than ever is it important to keep your expenses low and your investing high. Creating your own personal economy with assets can keep you from falling on hard times. You become your own bank when you have several pools to dip from.

Yale only puts 6% of its money in stock market. The Alternative Answer by Bob Rice is the first book to explain the new world of alternative investing strategies, showing how to use these new products for inflation-protected income, risk-adjusted growth, and long-term wealth transfer.

The Yale Endowment keeps only 6% of its investments in US stocks, but its portfolio has produced a 100% gain over the past decade. Indeed, the world's elite investors have long relied on alternative investments to produce their superior returns. Until now those options were the exclusive purview of institutions and the super wealthy, but today any informed investor can play the same game. A rainbow of investment options such as timber, startups, MLPs, hedged strategies, managed futures, infrastructure, cat bonds, peer-to-peer lending, farmland, and dozens of other non-traditional strategies can provide dramatically better gains, with less total risk, than the standard choices. In The Alternative Answer, Bob Rice, Bloomberg TV's Alternative Investment Editor, leads an entertaining and easy-to-understand tour of this world, and suggests specific alternative investments for all four key "jobs" of a portfolio: safely generating more current income; decreasing risks of economic shocks; significantly increasing long-term profits; and protecting purchasing power over time.

Regardless of experience or net worth, readers will learn exactly what to do to substantially improve their investment performance—in the same way that the world's best investors already do. Stocks and bonds alone aren't nearly enough. Investors need an Alternative Answer, and now they have it.

The average millionaire has 7 streams of income. Most common Farmland, Timber, Rental Income, Precious Metals, Dividend Income, Profit Income, Earned Income, and Insurance.

How many do you have?

Chapter 23

Farmland

"There are two spiritual dangers in not owning a farm. One is the danger of supposing that breakfast comes from the grocery, and the other that heat comes from the furnace."

— Aldo Leopold, *A Sand County Almanac*

"The ultimate goal of farming is not the growing of crops, but the cultivation and perfection of human beings."

— Masanobu Fukuoka, *The One-Straw Revolution*

"Teaching kids how to feed themselves and how to live in a community responsibly is the

center of an education."

— **Alice Waters**

The need for food is only increasing. United Kingdom and other Europeans countries are going all over Africa buying up farm land to keep up with the demand for food for its citizens. It's a real issue to suffer a food shortage so countries are becoming prepared. Chinese companies purchased the biggest pork provider smith field farms, and a huge chunk of farming companies.

How can little farmers compete in the wake of this? Selling organic products, creating farmers markets, making door to door deliveries. Pick and go locations.

Farming opportunities are greater than ever. The average American farmer is 65 years old. Soon to retire and leave our fields empty, the farm credit bureaus all around American are dumping millions into young, minority and women farmers.

You have a great time than ever to become a farmer or buy a large farmer and pay a small time farmer to manage it if you are not ready to return to the fields.

Farmers are now converting some of their land into winery, wedding event, cabins for Airbnb, homeaway and weekend getaways.

1) Is there a farming fruit or vegetable that interests you?

2) Have you thought about farming in retirement?

3) Have you thought about all the different opportunities farmland provides?

4) What is popular in your local farmers market?

5) What is your state or region known for?

Chapter 24

Timber

Timber is necessary for every country and production. It's important to own land that can produce different streams of income for you and just sell the trees off it if necessary.

What to do after you sale the trees off? Replant others and enjoy the benefits. There are many tax benefits to owning timber and farmland that produces income.

Examples of dividend stock

Lumber and wood production companies engage in the growing and harvesting of timber, along with the processing, distribution and sale of wood products. Lumber and wood production companies tend to be structured either as corporations or limited partnerships. These entities tend to offer dividend yields that are in-line with the market average. The table below has the stock name, price and dividend yield. Example KOP every $20 you put aside in KOP you will get a $1 back the end of the year. Imagine you saved $1000 dollars over the year you would receive $50 dollars back.

KOP

Koppers Holdings 5.00% $20.00 $1.00

CTT

CatchMark Timber Trust, Inc 4.48% $11.15 $0.50

POPE

Pope Resources L.P. 4.03% $64.55 $2.60

WY

Weyerhaeuser 3.74% $31.01 $1.16

MAS

Masco Corp. 1.35% $26.61 $0.36

UFPI

Universal Forest Products 1.27% $63.23 $0.80

AMWD

American Woodmark Corp 0.72% $65.08 $0.47

DEL

Deltic Timber 0.60% $66.55 $0.40

EVA

Enviva Partners, LP NA NA $3.16

(http://www.dividend.com/dividend-stocks/industrial-goods/lumber-wood-production/)

As an investment, timber is as boring as it gets. You're literally watching a tree grow. But that sleepy demeanor is exactly how the asset class benefits a portfolio. When lumber prices are low, timber companies can withhold harvesting logs and let the trees grow. When prices rise, they not only profit on the higher log price, but they make more money per tree since it is now larger. On average, a forest grows by about 7% each year.

That steady nature has made timberland a great investment over the long haul. (http://investorplace.com/2014/10/timber-reits-pch-ryn-wy/view-all/#.VcDfH_lViko)

My personal suggestion even if you owned 2 acres I would suggest you grow timber, or plant trees that can produce income in the future.

Chapter 25

Rental income

Investing is not risky. Investing is fun. Investing can make you very very rich. More importantly investing can set you free, free from the struggle of earning a living and worrying about money.

Robert Kiyosaki

As long as you have more cash flowing in than flowing out, your investment is a good investment.

Robert Kiyosaki

Keep it simple buy a house, move to another house. See the problem in America is we BUY too much house, then we cannot keep it and rent it out. Buying a house a year after year for 5 years is enough to buy most people freedom. Now these aren't A+++ houses maybe B or C houses, or duplexes.

Best example is afford anything blogger Paula Pant, who moved to Atlanta 5 years ago with just the backpack on her back. 5 years later she owns 7 rental properties. She was even able to buy houses cash. The house was $21,000 a year and she is receiving a $700-$900 rental monthly rental income from it. Imagine doing that 5 times you are getting $3500-$4500 a month.

Moving into a duplex or triplex almost guarantees you will live rent free for the time you are there. Use that rent free year (southeast) to save up income to invest in another duplex/triplex. It's a simple game of monopoly.

There are other ways to invest. REIT stocks that pay dividends. There are over 50 real estate crowdfunding sites and many you can invest in as little as $1000 to $5000 dollars.

Chapter 26

Precious metals

People seem to be extreme on one end or the other. I think precious metals actually in your hand is the best situation. China is buying up every piece of gold and silver they can get their hands on. China already put 5 billion on in US companies, land and real estate, now onto more gold.

Mining companies are going day and night to find more gold and silver. Reality TV shows made in Alaska, Africa and other places about men searching for gold.

Why is China buying up gold by the bucket loads? I think because other countries still see gold and silver as the "real" money. No matter how the United States says it's not, there is a reason India,

China, Brazil and other countries are trying to buy it by the truckloads.

From the Seeking Alpha article The Real Reason China Is Buying Up The World's Gold

- China's central bank is buying huge quantities of gold.
- China wants the yuan to become a reserve currency, but does not want a "strong yuan".
- China wants the leverage to control all currency values, which requires control of the gold market.

Chapter 27

Dividend income

If you are a true investor, it does not matter if the markets are going up or going down. A true investor does well in any market condition.

<u>Robert Kiyosaki</u>

Getting dividend income is simple as putting 100 a month away until you can just reinvest dividends and get results. You can reinvest dividends if you want. I know some people rather see in the mail a $20 dollar monthly check just to make sure the dividends are coming thru. The same is happening to millions of Florida retirees.

$1000 dollars will get you 20 dollars a month

back, depending on the stock. If you save up to 250,000 in dividend stock that's 5000 dollars monthly check hitting your mail box. Getting matched by your employer is a great way to get to $250,000. To accomplish this task in 10 years would require $25,000 saved a year for 10 years. $2,000 dollars put away a month.

$2000 dollars a month is too high for you even with your employer matching? We can break this down into a 20 year or 30 year career. Think about it if you are a police officer or military person deciding to finish out your career so you can get a pension or retirement package.

If you are going for a 30 year plan you will only need $700 a month for 30 years. Honestly half way through if you let the dividends reinvest about 10 years in you can let the dividends reinvest by itself.

Same for 20 years $1050 a month for 20 years, after about 10 years with $125,000 in the bank you will be receiving 2500 a month in dividends. You could completely stop investing after 10 years.

After 5 years of investing $1000 a month with 60,000 in the bank you would be receiving $1200 a month in dividend income. Imagine that 5 years into a job you thought you would love but now hate you can move on with a base of 1200 month income. You could achieve this same 5000 dollars a month by buying 3 fourplexes. 1 fourplex a year for 3 years. That's if each unit rented for $750 each a month.

Chapter 28

Profit income

"The Business of Our Firm is Business"
-Donald W. Hudspeth
"The Business of America is Business"
-Calvin Coolidge"

I have a guess on my slow and low series Youtube show Lamouris Thomas from Lousiana who never had a job at 24 years old he been selling atvs (four wheelers), scooters, and small motorcycles on Craigslist. Then he decided to go to the next level and private label over 7 items on amazon to increase his sales. He is surrounded by people who still hold jobs and haven't changed their thought process about making profit income.

Interesting through all his success his friends haven't followed his path. He is making money being his own boss yet they refuse to buck trends.

There is a 17 year old on YouTube who father gave her $250 dollars to buy items from china within 3 years she was making 1.2 million in sales. How can you change your life in 3 years? Your children and family probably have multiple ideas for reselling and making items to sell on line.

1) What are some ways you can make profit income?

2) What are some things you can pick up at a thift store today?

3) What are some items you would like to sell on Amazon?

4) What are some items you would like to sell on craigslist?

5) What are some items you would like to build a business around?

6) What are some things you can sell from around your home?

7) Are there yard sales or storage unit auctions near you?

8) Do you have a product you would like to sell?

Chapter 29

Earned income

Success requires discipline.

<u>Robert Kiyosaki</u>

Build up your earned income. If that means driving Uber/Lyft/rideshare on the weekends and building a business on the side do so. It's better to build a side business than get a second job. I only recommend folks getting a second job if they are trying to purchase real estate to live in or to rent out. Bankers like paperwork, so give them a bunch.

I want you to try and get the highest paying job possible or even a company that matches your 401K at 6%. Lowes Home Improvement even matched at

6%, but remember the average life span at a company is 2.5 years. Enjoy the match while possible and make sure to move 401K to a backup such as Edward Jones or such companies.

If you need income, like you will be homeless next month if you do not get your income up, then get a second job. I know several people telling me they cannot get a second job for schedule reasons, or some excuse. It's ridiculous you rather stay at your parents' house or live with roommates until you are 40.

Be honest with yourself. Do you want a better life? Do you want to travel? Do you want to live on your own?

I think the reason 1/3 of college educated and other young adults are living with their parents is because the lack of uncomfortableness. If your mom and dad were sick, unable to work and you were going to lose your child hood home and your parents I find this 1/3 would take on multiple jobs like immigrants do.

What is the made reasons Korean and Haitian immigrants become millionaires in 5 years of coming to the USA penniless? They work, they work everywhere. The founder of Forever 21 worked 3 jobs and his wife worked. Within 3 years he opened his first clothing store. How? He had a goal. He realized that coming to America was a golden ticket.

Hard work, works. I know many people leave in the inner city and have a hard time finding a job. This will require you to ride the bus a hour to the edges of the city to work, then you just do it. You do it until you can buy a car. Then when you buy the car, work and drive for Uber, Lyft or do deliver driving for pizza.

Here is the problem with that scenario, people do not want to work that hard. People think life is supposed to be easy. Why do I know that? People the amount of crying and whining about doing the right thing. People love telling everyone they are doing the right thing, but life isn't working out. Well keep trucking along because life is not fair.

It isn't people do not know what the right thing to do, its knowing what is the right thing for them.

1. What are you actions for the next 30 days?

2. The next 60 days?

3. The next 90 days?

4. What is your income outcome you are looking for?

Chapter 30

Insurance

Cash value

Reading the book millionaire by 30 I saw how adding money for 10 years to cash value life policy I could turnaround for the next 20 years and withdrawal 25000-50000 a year out to live off of. It would build up to a 1 million in value by 10 years.

Term

Basics if you can get an IPHONE or new car you can afford to send $40-$80 dollars a month for life insurance to cover your burial expenses and when you apply for business credit or a home mortgage you can show that you are a serious potential investor or client.

1) What time insurance do you need?

2) Who are you protecting with your insurance policy?

3) Can you afford to bury yourself today?

4) Why not borrow from yourself?

5) Is 10 years too long to invest in yourself?

Chaper 31

Tax Write-offs

I have a course on my website that list over 55 tax writes offs. I will not repeat all of them here. My goal is to direct you to a great CPA or accountant who can start working with your business in the early stages. They can find all the legal ways to get deductions, incentives and write-offs you need. A book I recommend is 1001 Business deductions and tax breaks. Each year they come out with a new model.

    Cell phones and Office land lines. People still confused on how cell phones are tax write-offs. Grab a second cheap $50 phone and use $45 dollar a month unlimited plan. You can write off this phone and all the activity on it. Stop using Google voice that has your personal line tied up.

There is an app called burner app, which gives you a different number as many as you want a month and you use it from your cell phone. It works great and I have texted from it. Gives you an extra layer of security and safety when calling clients, ordering things online, or even online dating.

Internet access. Wanting that $100-$200 a month internet plan? Get it. Show that you need it for business. There are even business phone and internet plans for your home.

Home office expenses outside of your desk, paper, computer you can include rent and utilities. Designate a room of your house to an office, and guess around ¼ of your utilities to the energy bills.

There are over 75 different tax write-offs

available to business owners. I meet folks daily who keep saying that the rich have tax loopholes. NO they do not, they have 1099 and businesses that are available for everyone.

Vacations while business is conducted. Youtube stars travel to several locations a year and do some videos while there. In essence they save 30% off their travel.

Chapter 32

Live well and teach others

"We cannot choose our circumstances, but we can choose how we handle them."
— Markus Pappa

Teach your children

I see so many families struggle financially generation after generation. Go to work because it was good enough for me mentality is not something to pass on to your children. If you will not grow yourself, at least make sure your children read, take interesting classes and test limits. It's really true your parents want a boring, safe life for you. Why because they love you. They want you not to fail, or get hurt. Guess what life is an adventure and not meant to be completely safe.

Many people tell their sons and daughters to open a business without how to do it, but just keep saying it. It allows the child to think about ways to do it. Dr Boyce Watkins says his father a police officer kept saying open a business and it made the idea grow.

Keeping one job for 40 years and then retiring is a thing of the past. Your kids will need to learn about stocks, investing, real estate and multiple streams of income. Encourage your kids to read millionaire by 30, take a course on investing, and work in the meantime.

Backwards planning is so important. If you kid wants to make $5,000 a month to cover debt and travel, they need to understand how many hours of work that will take or how many sales. Once I saw a few sales from my online business, I realize what amount of marketing and sales I needed to live well. The people you see continuously traveling keep their debt expenses low.

Chapter 33

Teach 10 others

Can you imagine is you teach 10 people and they go on to teach 10 others *each. That is 100 homes, families, and businesses that have been affected by your decision. My goal is to grow 100,000 1099 classy climbers. I know if I teach a room full of 100-250 people at a time and they all teach 100 others that's 10,000-25,000 lives changed. I could do teach 100-250 ten times and my dream could come true.

These people could fix unemployment in their cities and towns. They could help relatives get jobs, they could grow their businesses to new levels. It's possible. If the kids get a mental map in their communities about what is possible they can reach for new heights.

Make YouTube videos so people know there is freedom outside an office. The more 1099 entrepreneur lifestyle videos the better. Look at the Tim Ferris 4 hour work week bandwagon, it open people's eyes to other lifestyles. On top of that I have met people who have no clue what 4 hour work week even is. There is room in the marketplace for you.

Made in the USA
Columbia, SC
10 March 2018